Dr. DooRiddles
B2
Associative Reasoning Activities

Series Titles
Dr. DooRiddles A1, A2, A3, B1, B2, C1
Spelling DooRiddles A1, B1

John H. Doolittle
&
Tracy A. Doolittle

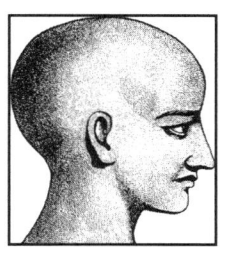

© 2005
THE CRITICAL THINKING CO.™
Phone: 800-458-4849 Fax: 831-393-3277
www.CriticalThinking.com
P.O. Box 1610 • Seaside • CA 93955-1610
ISBN 978-0-89455-879-5

The individual who purchases this book is licensed to reproduce the student pages for use within his or her classroom or home. This reproduction license is limited to one home or one classroom. No reproduction rights are granted to any commercial entity or organization without the expressed written consent of The Critical Thinking Co.™
Printed in the United States of America

ABOUT THE AUTHOR

John Doolittle has been a professor of psychology at California State University, Sacramento since 1966. He received a bachelor's degree in biology and psychology from Stanford University, a master's degree in psychology from San Jose State University, and a doctoral degree in experimental psychology from the University of Colorado, Boulder. At Sacramento, Dr. Doolittle has taught in the schools of Education, Arts and Sciences, and Engineering and Computer Science. He has also been a visiting professor at the University of Melbourne, Australia. Dr. Doolittle is the author of a number of books and software published by The Critical Thinking Co.™, including *Riddle Mysteries* software, *Dr. DooRiddles*, and *Spelling DoRiddles*.

When Tracy A. Doolittle is not writing riddles, she works for KVIE public television and is pursuing a Masters degree in English at CSU, Sacramento.

TEACHER SUGGESTIONS

Everyone loves the mystery of a riddle and *Dr. DooRiddles* will bring laughter, groans, and challenges (perhaps for as much as a week or more per riddle) to you and your students.

Thinking Skills

Perceiving relationships between words, ideas, and concepts is called associative reasoning, which is a skill necessary for creative thought. Riddle solving requires students to use important skills of associative, inductive, and divergent thinking to find the answers. Students will learn to recognize important ideas, examine these ideas from different points of view, and then find connections between the ideas. These teachable skills are essential for efficient, successful, open-ended problem solving of all kinds.

Role of the Student

Although *Dr. DooRiddles* are fun and tantalizing, answering them is not simple play. In order to solve these riddles, students have to generate solutions in many different categories. Students often confuse a multiple-category generation of answers with offering the same answer rephrased. To clarify this confusion, students need to learn how to examine an idea from many reference points.

For Example: If one of the given clues in a riddle were the word *horn*, students would have to think of different meanings and applications of that word. Does it refer to a kind of musical instrument? a part of an animal? to the geographic term? a general horn shape? or does it refer to an alternative in a dilemma?

Role of the Teacher

At first, the teacher will need to help the students learn how to produce multiple-category solutions by asking higher level thinking questions. Eventually, responsibility of self-questioning should be turned over to the students. Teach your students to ask themselves questions such as:

- How is the clue used?
- Why is it phrased this way?
- Is this clue connected to a clue in another line?
- How else can this word be spelled?
- Is this a whole word or a partial word?
- Does this line mean what it says or is it a play on words?
- Does this word sound like another word?

Students should be encouraged to "listen" to the riddles, examining the sound of each line and individual words, and to use visual imagery to "see" what's happening. As they get into the process of riddle solving, they will learn to read and weigh the importance of each word in each line so they can interpret the clues correctly. They will learn to notice how highly descriptive adjectives, verbs, and adverbs indicate specific kinds of movement or action; and how unusual phonetic spellings, homonyms, prefixes, suffixes, roots, puns, analogies, and multiple word meanings are used to both hide and reveal the clues.

Dr. DooRiddles B2 — Answers

Always ask students why they chose the answer they did. Do not allow students to just give their answer without explaining the reasoning behind it. When answers are backed up and evaluated in group discussions, class members share their knowledge, connect it to other ideas and explore the concept in many directions to find a "best" answer from among possible multiple answers. By working and sharing information in groups, children who are not familiar with the culture, or who lack English proficiency, will expand their knowledge, build more extensive vocabulary, and will be able to apply information more diversely.

Classroom Application

These materials make great sponge activities and are excellent activities for independent, cooperative, or open learning situations. The riddles can be used as part of the daily thinking skill curriculum or for the challenge of the week. The riddles spiral up in difficulty within each book and from level to level so that teachers may select the appropriate level of difficulty for students.

Dr. DooRiddles cuts across curriculum areas and deals with real-world objects and situations. Both teachers and students will find the mind-broadening strategies used in these challenging activities richly rewarding at test-taking time.

ANSWERS

Page 1
- skeleton
- parachute, parakeet
- rich

Page 2
- piggy bank, bank robber
- strike
- stage coach, coach

Page 3
- tree
- gold
- gate

Page 4
- garage
- plate, home plate
- fool

Page 5
- careful, carriage
- blew, blue
- strawberry, blackberry, blueberry, bury

Page 6
- cash, cashew
- forecast, castaway
- boardwalk, sidewalk

Page 7
- irregular, earlobe
- flag
- tornado, torn

Page 8
- sock
- post
- rap, wrap

Page 9
- can
- table
- bow

Page 10
- catch
- bird
- train

Page 11
- light
- spell
- corn

Page 12
- sand
- skates
- chicken

Page 13
- ice
- address
- grand

Page 14
- whole, hole
- iron
- laps

Page 15
- mold
- notes, note
- nuts, nut

Page 16
- pack
- bye, buy
- letters

Page 17
- march, March
- medal, metal
- eight, ate

Page 18
- fall
- fan
- fine

Page 19
- fire
- forth, fourth
- frame

Page 20
- hide
- pouring
- beg

Page 21
- question
- rain, reign
- tender, ten

Page 22
- vain, vein
- log, log on, log in

Dr. DooRiddles B2 — Answers

-satellite, saddle

Page 23
- pansy, panda, panic
- mistake, ache
- cover, discover

Page 24
- tray, traitor
- pound
- say, sail

Page 25
- pad, paddle
- granite, granule, granola
- dull, handle, candle

Page 26
- overheard, herd
- miss
- well

Page 27
- witness, whittle
- jam
- move, remove

Page 28
- saves
- trapeze, trap
- peanuts, people

Page 29
- pharaoh, fair
- liver, deliver
- dart

Page 30
- course
- discus, compact disk
- castaway, getaway

Page 31
- notion, lotion, ocean
- c, sea, see
- dreams, sleep

Page 32
- sink
- finish
- inc., ink

Page 33
- off, office
- race
- marry, merry

Page 34
- hours, ours
- jar
- mistake, mist

Page 35
- page
- pants
- base, bass

Page 36
- mark
- coarse, course
- fair

Page 37
- felt
- flop
- form

Page 38
- rose
- rough, ruff
- seem, seam

Page 39
- aimless, aim

- outstanding, outside
- true

Page 40
- airy, dictionary
- laps, collapse
- normal, ignore

Page 41
- persuade, purse
- finance, fine
- stash, mustache

Page 42
- pass, passenger
- attendance, attend
- force

Page 43
- hitchhike, hitch
- petals, pedals
- seen, scene

Page 44
- layer, lair
- post, post office
- chip

Page 45
- feet, feat
- fence
- habit

Page 46
- hopeless, hope
- seal
- joking, king

Page 47
- junk
- secret, seek
- warrant, warble

Page 48
- evidence
- classical, class
- novelty, novel

Page 49
- bumble, bumper
- brewing, brunette, brutal
- baron, barren

Page 50
- seize, seas
- typewriter, stereotype
- warn, worn

Page 51
- turn
- soil, boil, toil
- orchid, orchard, order

Page 52
- just
- cross
- leaf

Page 53
- fit
- flee, flea
- green, green giant, green grass

Page 54
- higher, hire

MODEL LESSON

My tail can wag,
My feet there are four;
I scratch or bark,
When I want out the door.

Each line, or pair of lines, in the above riddle contains a clue to the answer. Carefully read each line and try to figure out what is being described. Look for clue words. Try to form a picture in your mind as you connect all the clues. Ask yourself questions about each of the clues.

For Example:

> In the first line, *tail* and *wag* are clue words. What has a tail and wags it?
>
> In the second line, *four feet* are clue words. What has four feet and a tail that can wag?
>
> In the third line, *scratch* and *bark* are clue words. What scratches and barks?
>
> In the fourth line, *want out the door* goes with scratch and bark. What scratches and barks when it wants out the door?

Now how would you connect all the clues? Perhaps the first thing that comes to mind as an answer is a dog. Let's see if dog works. A dog does have a tail, and it wags it when it is happy. A dog does have four feet. When a dog wants to go out, it often scratches or barks to let its owner know. So dog does fit all the clues and it is a good answer. Someone else may come up with a different answer, and if it fits all the clues, it is also a good answer.

I'm a person made of bones,
A fright at Halloween;
The structure of a body,
With nothing in between.

What am I? ....

With chute I will help,
If you jump from a plane;
With keet a small bird,
Whose feathers aren't plain.

What am I? ....

Another word for wealthy,
To have lots of money;
Or a delicious dessert,
That fills up your tummy.

What am I? ....

With piggy,
I hold change that is loose;
With robber,
I watch out for the noose.

What am I? ....

In bowling I'm pins,
Flying off here and there;
In lightning I'm bolts,
So picnickers beware!

What am I? ....

With stage I'm your ride,
Across the old frontier;
Alone I'm the one,
The players hold so dear.

What am I? ....

My family is your folks,
And their folks and so on;
Alone I have a big trunk,
That leaves and bark grow on.

What am I? ....

I'm panned for in rivers,
And discovered on land;
Or found on your finger,
In a circular band.

What am I? ....

A door that's like a fence,
I'll keep in the dog;
Sometimes made of iron,
Or wood from a log.

What am I? ....

Leave your car in me,
But first check the lock;
A place for a sale,
You have on your block.

What am I? ....

Think first of the dish,
That holds your dinner;
Or think of the home,
Crossed by the winner.

What am I? ....

A person with no sense,
Which means he is not wise;
Or else to trick your friend,
By wearing a disguise.

What am I? ....

With full I mean that you,
Proceed so cautiously;
With rage I'm a wagon,
That queens ride graciously.

What am I? ....

They say huffed, puffed and I,
Did bring the pig's house down;
A color in the flag,
That flies above our town.

What am I? ....

Now, straw and black and blue,
Will all go well with me;
Do me to the treasure,
In sand quite near the sea.

What am I? ....

Another word for money,
That banks keep in a vault;
With ew I become a nut,
That's really good with salt.

What am I? ....

With fore I'm the weather,
That's coming tomorrow;
With away I'm stranded,
And feeling some sorrow.

What am I? ....

With board I am boards,
A carnival stroll;
With side I'm cement,
Where bikes shouldn't go.

What am I? ....

With regular I'm not,
So regular at all;
With lobe I am a place,
For earrings large and small.

What am I? ....

To wave someone down,
When you need some helping hands;
A symbol that flies,
And represents different lands.

What am I? ....

With *naydo* I am wind,
I swirl and I scare;
Alone those pages,
Are no longer there.

What am I? ....

A big kid just hit you,
And your arm is still sore;
Or clothing for your feet,
You don't leave on the floor.

What am I? ....

A card whose message,
Is not very long;
I hold up the fence,
And help keep it strong.

What am I? ....

A name for the music,
With more talk than song;
Or else the covering,
That makes food last long.

What am I? ....

What word means able,
To do it yourself?
Or a house for the soup,
That sits on the shelf.

What am I? ....

What thing has four legs,
But it doesn't walk?
Something to write on,
And eat at and talk.

What am I? ....

A present all wrapped
Then ribbon you tie;
With rain see a colorful,
Arch in the sky.

What am I? ....

A tug on the line,
Means here comes the fish;
If a ball's coming at you,
It's yours, if you wish.

What am I? ....

The big guy you see,
On Sesame Street;
The feathery things,
That like to go "tweet."

What am I? ....

The kind of vehicle,
That keeps you on track;
Or else, daily workouts,
If speed's what you lack.

What am I? ....

What a thing must be,
If lifting it's easy;
Or what matches do,
If it's not too breezy.

What am I? ....

Tell me in order,
The letters in "road";
A witch would use me,
To make you a toad.

What am I? ....

From out in the fields,
Popped in for a snack;
And though I have ears,
It's hearing I lack.

What am I? ....

I'm tiny rocks on the beach,
Where people's skin turns red;
With wich I'm peanut butter,
Beween two slabs of bread.

What am I? ....

On my wheels or blades,
You glide or you wobble;
Wear lots of padding,
Just in case of trouble.

What am I? ....

I'm eaten fried,
Good taste hot or cold;
And do you know,
Why I crossed the road?

What am I? ....

I make your drink colder,
And, then, melt away;
With cream I taste yummy,
On a warm summer's day.

What am I? ....

I'm numbers and some words,
Used to locate your home;
Give me to the police,
If you should stray or roam.

What am I? ....

I am large or worthy,
I'm elegant, not bad;
With mother I'm mom's mom,
With father I'm dad's dad.

What am I? ....

I'm all complete,
No piece to take;
In the ground I'm,
Home to a snake.

What am I? ....

Take that wrinkled shirt,
And smooth out the creases;
Or I'm a metal,
Whose strength never ceases.

What am I? ....

Swimming in the pool,
From this end to that;
When you were a kid,
These are where you sat.

What am I? ....

Green and black I grow,
On really old bread;
Or to shape into,
Something else instead.

What am I? ....

Many of me,
Will make up a song;
Or a message,
Please pass it along.

What am I? ....

You're acting crazy,
You're acting like me;
I'm a crunchy treat,
That grows on a tree.

What am I? ....

Put trip clothes in a case,
For all kinds of weather;
Or wolves in the wild,
Hanging out together.

What am I? ....

The good thing you say,
Walking out the door;
Getting what you want,
From your favorite store.

What am I? ....

You might use me,
To spell any word;
Through mail I bring,
The news you've not heard.

What am I? ....

In two straight lines,
Soldiers move down the lane;
The month before,
The one that brings the rain.

What am I? ....

When you've won the big race,
Around your neck I'm worn;
I'm iron, steel or I'm,
The brass in that French horn.

What am I? ....

Think of me as four,
With four more added on;
The fate of the food,
That once was there and now gone.

What am I? ....

When the leaves shine red,
And orange on the trees;
The stumble that brings,
You down to your knees.

What am I? ....

I move the air,
To keep you feeling cool;
One that likes you,
And cheers your team at school.

What am I? ....

Hair that is thin,
And soft to the touch;
Feeling okay,
Not bothered by much.

What am I? ....

What a boss might do,
When he wants you to go;
Or a source of heat,
When the wind starts to blow.

What am I? ....

With brought I am something,
Pushed up from the back;
Or the one after third,
That's next in the stack.

What am I? ....

To make them all think,
That he did the crime;
Around your photos,
Or painting that's fine.

What am I? ....

A skin that is stitched,
To make simple clothes;
With seek I'm a game,
Where am I? Who knows!

What am I? ....

From milk to the glass,
I'm the action you take;
When it's raining hard,
Stay dry for goodness sake!

What am I? ....

What a dog does,
For scraps at the table;
To say please, please,
Please if you are able.

What am I? ....

So many things to ask,
And doing so may cause a spark;
When you need an answer,
Finish the sentence with my mark.

What am I? ....

My drops hit the soil,
And plants grow up green;
Or the time of royal rule,
By a king or a queen.

What am I? ....

With der I'm not tough,
Not cruel nor mean;
Alone I'm not twelve,
Or nine, but between!

What am I? ....

A person so proud,
I love myself so;
Or a tube for blood,
So that it can flow.

What am I? ....

Use me and some dry kindling,
To make a fire bright;
With on or in you'll enter,
That great computer site.

What am I? ....

My lite flies in space,
Telling us about rain;
Alone I'm your seat,
Riding out on the plain.

What am I? ....

With zee I'm a flower,
With duh I'm a bear;
With nick you will want,
To get out of there!

What am I? ....

With mist I am an error,
Erase me and I'm gone;
Alone I am a dull pain,
That just goes on and on.

What am I? ....

Don't judge a book by me,
That saying is quite true;
With dis I mean to find,
Something that's new to you.

What am I? ....

Alone I can hold drinks,
Or a nice tea set;
With tor I'm disloyal,
How low can you get?

What am I? ....

Though I'm not a number,
I'm a key on a phone;
A unit of measure,
That tells how much you've grown.

What am I? ....

Alone I mean to speak,
I do not mean to write;
With ul I push the boat,
If the wind is just right.

What am I? ....

For launching a rocket,
I am just the site;
For moving a canoe,
My dull works just right.

What am I? ....

With it I am rock,
With yule I am small;
With ola I'm oats,
To help you grow tall.

What am I? ....

Alone I'm not sharp,
I'm boring, yes quite;
With hand I am turned,
With can I'm a light.

What am I? ....

With over I'm what,
You did hear people say;
Alone I'm a bunch,
Of cows out to graze.

What am I? ....

I'm never a hit,
A mark not met;
I'm a young woman,
Not married yet.

What am I? ....

The bucket goes down,
And up comes a drink;
If you're me, you're not sick,
You're sure in the pink.

What am I? ....

With ness I testify,
To all I've seen and heard;
With tull I carve the wood,
And it becomes a bird.

What am I? ....

With traffic I'm stuck,
In a line of cars;
Alone I'm a spread,
Often found in jars.

What am I? ....

Alone I mean to go,
And live some other place;
With re I mean to take,
I'm somewhat like erase.

What am I? ....

She puts all her earnings,
Into her piggy bank;
And rescues that young boy,
Seconds before he sank!

What am I? ....

With ease I go flying,
Higher than a house;
Alone I am holding,
That poor little mouse.

What am I? ....

With nuts but not with bolts,
I make a tasty treat;
With pull I am the folks,
Who live along the street.

What am I? ....

With oh I'm a mummy,
A king who's long dead;
Alone I am weather,
That looks good ahead.

What am I? ....

I'm a body organ,
You need to stay alive;
With de they take what's sent,
And help it to arrive.

What am I? ....

I'm thrown at a target,
I'm a sharp, little arrow;
Or I move very quickly,
Think hummingbird or sparrow.

What am I? ....

I am the path or route,
That his ship takes to shore;
A place where golfers play,
And swing and holler, "fore!"

What am I? ....

My cuss doesn't swear,
But flies through the air;
My compact has sounds,
Stored on it with care.

What am I? ....

With cast I'm all alone,
This island is my jail;
With get I'm on the run,
With anchors we set sail.

What am I? ....

With no I'm a thought,
With lo I'm a balm;
With o I'm the sea,
We hope will stay calm.

What am I? ....

A popular letter,
Or larger than a lake;
Or the thing that you do,
When a look you take.

What am I? ....

A far, far off land,
That's filled with excitement;
But, then you sit up,
And wonder where night went.

What am I? ....

A place for dishes,
But they shouldn't stay;
Or what a rock does,
When thrown in the bay.

What am I? ....

First, I am the shine,
That wax seems to grace;
Or think of the line,
That must end the race.

What am I? ....

I'm the abbreviation,
You see in company names;
Or what the pens must use,
To write about the games.

What am I? ....

Alone I am not on,
A switch that's pointing down;
With iss I am a room,
Where people work downtown.

What am I? ....

A way to group people,
That's done harm in the past;
Or else I'm a contest,
To find out who is fast.

What am I? ....

Think first of a wedding,
A groom and a bride;
Then think of a jolly,
And happy sleigh ride.

What am I? ....

Shown by the clock,
I'm a piece of time;
Together I'm,
His, hers, yours, and mine.

What am I? ....

To awaken something,
With a shake or a nudge;
I've a mouth and a lid,
And can hold some hot fudge.

What am I? ....

With ache I'm a choice,
You've come to regret;
I'm lighter than rain,
But still leave you wet.

What am I? ....

Turn me when,
Reading stories of lore;
Hear me if,
You are lost in the store.

What am I? ....

A thirsty dog,
With his tongue hanging low;
Not quite your jeans,
More like trousers, you know?

What am I? ....

A corner of the diamond,
In a sport we all know;
Or I am a singing voice,
That's very, very low.

What am I? ....

You stand on me,
Before "get set" and "go"!
Your paper's grade,
Whether it's high or low.

What am I? ....

Having no manners,
Or fabric that is rough;
That one class at school,
You think is kind of tough.

What am I? ....

An outdoor celebration,
With music and pies;
Or a pale, freckled beauty,
With powder blue eyes.

What am I? ....

A soft bit of fabric,
Perhaps for a hat?
Or to have touched something,
A couch or a cat.

What am I? ....

You fall on your belly,
Into the water that's cold;
A play that closes from,
No tickets being sold.

What am I? ....

The new shape that it takes,
When it once was a blob;
The paper you fill out,
Applying for a job.

What am I? ....

What you did when,
You stood from that chair;
Or a bright flower,
Whose scent fills the air.

What am I? ....

A surface that's not smooth,
Something not nice to touch;
Or the sound the dog makes,
To say he likes you much.

What am I? ....

What appears to be true,
The impression you got;
Or where fabric is stitched,
The line that marks the spot.

What am I? ....

With less I wander,
Not going left or right;
I am what you take,
When a target's in sight.

What am I? ....

With standing you did well,
Yes, you were very good;
With side you're on the lawn,
Or standing in the wood.

What am I? ....

I never can be false,
Or accused of misdirection;
My love is forever,
With sweetness and affection.

What am I? ....

Alone I am light,
And lofty and breezy;
With diction a home,
For words hard and easy.

What am I? ....

Alone back and forth,
You paddle the pool;
With col I mean things,
Have just fallen through.

What am I? ....

With mull I am average,
Conforming to convention;
With ig I'm neglecting,
And paying no attention.

What am I? ....

With wade I am words,
That sound so appealing;
Alone, hold my strap,
In case folks are stealing.

What am I? ....

My ance has to do,
With banking and such;
Or overdue books,
For which you'll pay much.

What am I? ....

Alone I am stuff,
That's hidden away;
With muss I am hair,
He won't have to shave.

What am I? ....

A football that is thrown,
To someone near or far;
With uhnjur I will ride,
But will not drive the car.

What am I? ....

My ance will be taken,
Each day at the school;
Alone I mean focus,
And don't gather wool.

What am I? ....

The police have this,
When you see two, ten, or more;
The strength you need,
To open that stubborn door.

What am I? ....

My hike is all thumbs,
Without much shoe wear;
I cause the trailer,
To follow you there.

What am I? ....

I'm part of what's seen,
On a flowering bush;
I sound like the things,
That car drivers must push.

What am I? ....

Here's a verb for the eyes,
Whose tense is now past;
A beautiful setting,
That you hope will last.

What am I? ....

A cake piled high,
Has many of me;
A lion's den,
You might want to flee!

What am I? ....

Sometimes made of wood,
Onto me the fence is nailed;
My office is where,
All your packages are mailed.

What am I? ....

A teacup that's broken,
It's missing a chunk;
A crisp, salty snack,
In some dip you will dunk!

What am I? ....

Something to tackle,
That is big and taxing;
Or two that are bare,
When you are relaxing.

What am I? ....

A clashing of swords,
To parry or to spar;
Or what you might climb,
To reach places afar.

What am I? ....

You've gotten used to,
The way that it's done;
The black and the white,
Clothing of a nun.

What am I? ....

With less I bring sadness,
Seems there's no way out;
Alone I can cheer you,
Erasing that doubt.

What am I? ....

To close the box,
For sending in the mail;
Found in the sea,
But smaller than a whale.

What am I? ....

With joke I amuse,
The group that now listens;
Alone I shall rule,
With a crown that glistens.

What am I? ....

Oh, my food may taste good,
But it will make you plump;
Or I am useless stuff,
That will go to the dump.

What am I? ....

With rit I'm concealed,
Let no one else know;
Alone I am looking,
I search high and low.

What am I? ....

With rent I'm a paper,
To bring someone in;
With bull I'm a nice song,
Of robin or wren.

What am I? ....

My overall weight,
Must be quite substantial;
With witnesses, words,
And facts circumstantial.

What am I? ....

With sickle I am music,
To which few kids relate;
Alone I am people,
With whom you'll graduate.

What am I? ....

With tea I am new,
A treat and a change;
Alone I'm a book,
With many a page.

What am I? ....

My bull is all thumbs,
Or a bee who stings;
With per I save cars,
From dents and from dings.

What am I? ....

With ing I'm a tea bag,
In water that's hot;
With net I'm hair color,
With tull nice I'm not.

What am I? ....

I'm not quite a duke,
Or even an earl;
Or somewhere so bare,
You won't see a squirrel.

What am I? ....

A word that means grab,
To take without asking;
Or think of oceans,
Beside which you're basking.

What am I? ....

A writer you just don't,
See much of these days;
A stereo that's not,
Fair to any race.

What am I? ....

When you say "Be careful",
What is it you do?
Or how do we speak of,
That hole in your shoe?

What am I? ....

If you both can't use it,
You have to take me;
Or earth on its axis,
Does me constantly.

What am I? ....

With S I am called dirt,
With B the water's hot;
With T you work so hard,
That you may pant a lot.

What am I? ....

With kid a flower sweet,
With churd a grove of trees;
With der you ask for fries,
As always you say please.

What am I? ....

A person with morals,
In other words, fair;
Or almost within reach,
But still not quite there.

What am I? ....

When I'm red I help,
Those who are in need;
Alone I'm bitter,
And angry indeed.

What am I? ....

To flip through the pages,
Of a book or magazine;
I can change my color,
To red, orange, or just stay green.

What am I? ....

You're in good shape,
Look at those thighs!
The pants that are,
Just the right size.

What am I? ....

To leave the scene,
On foot or by car;
That biting bug,
You know who you are.

What am I? ....

A way to say,
You're a novice or new;
The giant tall,
Or the grass topped with dew.

What am I? ....

I'm somewhere above,
Where you are now;
You're given the job,
Go take a bow.

What am I? ....